T0207724

Read the Reviews!

Divine Directions from the Car Seat is a delightful book of daily meditations inspired by a grandma's conversations and experiences with her granddaughter. Common daily occurrences have been insightfully applied to spiritual truths. Questions for reflection are also provided to encourage personal, practical application. This is a refreshing approach for our devotional lives.

—Kirkie Morrissey, author and Bible teacher

"You have taught children and infants of your strength," says Psalm 8:2 (NLT). Debbie has heeded these words, listened for God's voice during times with her granddaughter, and now shares thought-provoking insights for daily living. Relatable stories and additional helps urge us to reflect upon what God has to say to each of us.

—Marian Stryker, early childhood development teacher

I will never see another grilled cheese sandwich in the same way again! Inspired by God, this is a must-read for grandparents, grandchildren, and anyone who desires a delicious way to start the day.

—Lee Wagman, president and CEO,
Personality Resources International, LLC

Simple but so profound! As a new father, Debbie has helped me appreciate this season with my daughter as I venture to love and lead her little life. At the same time, this book allows me to understand that dad too is being taught valuable life and spiritual lessons along this joyful journey.

—Major Daniel Walker, military chaplain

Divine Directions from the Car Seat

Thirty-One Meditations from God through Reagan to Me and Now to You

DEBORAH DENISON BAILEY

WESTBOW
PRESS®
A DIVISION OF THOMAS NELSON
& ZONDERVAN

This book is a work of non-fiction. Unless otherwise noted, the author and the publisher make no explicit guarantees as to the accuracy of the information contained in this book and in some cases, names of people and places have been altered to protect their privacy.

WestBow Press books may be ordered through booksellers or by contacting:

WestBow Press
A Division of Thomas Nelson & Zondervan
1663 Liberty Drive
Bloomington, IN 47403
www.westbowpress.com
1 (866) 928-1240

Because of the dynamic nature of the Internet, any web addresses or links contained in this book may have changed since publication and may no longer be valid. The views expressed in this work are solely those of the author and do not necessarily reflect the views of the publisher, and the publisher hereby disclaims any responsibility for them.

Any people depicted in stock imagery provided by Getty Images are models, and such images are being used for illustrative purposes only.
Certain stock imagery © Getty Images.

Scripture taken from the Holy Bible, NEW INTERNATIONAL VERSION®. Copyright © 1973, 1978, 1984, 2011 by Biblica, Inc. All rights reserved worldwide. Used by permission. NEW INTERNATIONAL VERSION® and NIV® are registered trademarks of Biblica, Inc. Use of either trademark for the offering of goods or services requires the prior written consent of Biblica US, Inc.

Images on pages 81 and 99 by Megan Denison Smith@2019.

ISBN: 978-1-9736-7340-8 (sc)
ISBN: 978-1-9736-7341-5 (hc)
ISBN: 978-1-9736-7339-2 (e)

Library of Congress Control Number: 2019913747

Print information available on the last page.

WestBow Press rev. date: 10/24/2019

*To my granddaughter, Reagan Marie, who has expanded
my world beyond measure. And when she is able to
read, I hope this book will do the same for her.*

*To my mother, Rachel Crittenden Denison,
who always wanted to write a book.*

Reagan Marie Bailey in her car seat!

Contents

Each one of these meditations is about living life to the fullest, learning all we can about our Maker, glorifying Him, and spreading the good news! Grandparents and grandchildren enjoy a special bond, which makes growing in the Lord together even more exciting!

"Honey, life is for the living!"
—Bill Denison, my father

Preface

When Reagan Marie was born in the fall of 2013, the world was forever changed for my husband and me. Now proudly known as Nana and Bampa, we have enjoyed the tremendous blessing of loving our precious granddaughter. She is our shining star who has made His light brighter in our lives.

When Reagan began to talk, I started writing down some things that she said because I felt they would be important family keepsakes. As time has gone by, I have sensed that the Lord wanted me to use her words for His glory. I have learned along the way that the innocent remarks of a child can have a profound and lasting impact, particularly when we apply that insight into our daily lives. I am reminded of the scripture from Isaiah 11:6, "and a child shall lead them," which has certainly been the case here.

It is to honor Christ and spread His message that I have written these thirty-one meditations. I feel absolutely certain that the Lord Himself spoke through Reagan to me, and now they are provided for your reflection.

May you be blessed and feel His Spirit as you navigate through these meditations. I invite you to enjoy the ride as we follow His divine direction from Reagan's car seat.

1 | Steps

May 5, 2015

We often use the images of baby steps and giant steps when describing our spiritual growth. I am not sure, however, when I last marveled about actual steps—the up-and-down kind. As I have watched Reagan take absolute delight in going from one level to another, it has caused me to smile, pause, and reflect.

When we go to the outdoor playground, there is a slight shift in elevation from the sand to the rubber mats on top of the sand. There is also a small difference between the grass and the sidewalk and from the cover of the water sprinkler in the grass to the grass—tiny height differences. Yet eighteen-month-old Reagan takes great enjoyment in continuously stepping back and forth from one level to the other. Why? There does not appear to be any challenge involved. But she squeals with glee as she maneuvers, ever so slightly, back and forth and up and down. Even through her sturdy sneakers the ground must feel different. The outcome is always successful—never falling and always wanting to do it again.

We are all like that in many ways. We also like to be successful. We like the feel of a good experience, so we repeat it. The differences between Reagan's encounter and ours are our age and our parameters. Our innocence has faded. Our satisfaction in doing simple things seems to diminish with time. Rather than taking pleasure in doing the same thing, the repetition often bores us. Besides, what is the big deal about steps?

Frequently when spiritual assessments are offered, a question is asked about where we are on the growth ladder. Are we close to the bottom or near the top? If there are ten rungs to the spiritual ladder, we generally are content to be at the fifth or sixth step because we ask, "What is really the big deal about steps?"

Again I think about Reagan and her excitement as she shifts back and forth on the elevation differences of the ground. My first step was to invite Christ into my life. For sure, that was a squealy, delightful moment! And now, as I attempt to advance to the next heights, I want to have that same enthusiasm about my spiritual growth. Like Reagan, I want to never tire and always be enthusiastic as I move forward and look back with a grateful heart.

Key Thought

Be excited about each step, no matter how slight.

Scripture

"Since we live by the Spirit, let us be in step with the Spirit" (Galatians 5:25).

Prayer

Father, thank You for all the opportunities to grow in Your Spirit. Thank You for guiding our steps and enabling us to have just enough courage to take the next step at all times and in all circumstances. We take pleasure in and are grateful for Your provision. Thank You for reminders like the excitement we see in children's eyes. May we approach You with that same kind of anticipation as we venture to take each step. In Your name we pray. Amen.

For Further Reflection

1. On a spiritual ladder that has ten rungs, where are you on the ladder? Explain.
2. What steps do you routinely take to be in step with the Spirit?
3. We all struggle with the challenges that daily life brings. How do you address those issues?
4. Do you consciously endeavor to maintain an enthusiasm for all things great and small? How?

2 | Brave

July 23, 2015

The first thunderstorm that Reagan and I experienced together was both partly exciting and scary as well as totally endearing. It will always be a sweet and precious memory—perhaps for both of us.

Boom! Crash! Crack! The thunder and lightning were relentless for a very long hour. Reagan and I frequently exclaimed one of our favorite words—"Yikes!"—as the room shook when we heard the thunder. Huddled together in my bed, we summoned our courage to look toward the window in my bedroom as the torrential rain pounded against the panes. Each time there was lightning, the room lit up. This was a big storm! When the rage of the storm began, I gently told Reagan that she was brave.

The storm is long gone now, but each time Reagan looks at that window, she is reminded of the stormy blast and says, "Brave." It was a frightening experience that she remembers as the time when she was brave. Now also, whenever Reagan hears thunder, she says, "Brave." That is often followed by an ever so slight whimper, and then she nestles her head into my shoulder. When she sees clouds forming, she clenches her fists and then bumps them together while explaining that she understands about thunder. She proudly demonstrates that the thundering sound is made when the clouds bump into each other. That is followed again by a slight whimper as she puts her chin to her chest, looks up with her eyes, and softly yet courageously says, "Brave!"

As Reagan and I repeat this endearing ritual, it prompts me to stop and consider the way we all do the same thing. We hold our breath as we summon our courage, maybe even clench our fists, and then, if we are wise, we go racing into our heavenly Father's arms. Nestled there in our weakness, we are given strength to be brave. Whenever we make the bold choice to empty ourselves and yield to His power, we are brave!

I pray that as Reagan gets older, she will realize that whatever storms come her way, her Father, God Almighty, will hold her and she will be empowered to be brave through His strength.

Key Thought

God is with us through the storms.

Scripture

"For when I am weak, then I am strong" (2 Corinthians 12:1).

Prayer

Dear heavenly Lord, You are our strength at all times and in all ways. You are our refuge, our hiding place, and the source of all power and might. May we always remember to give You the glory for who You are in every circumstance of our lives. Thank You for Your loving arms that hold us and protect us. In the name of Jesus Christ, we pray. Amen.

For Further Reflection

1. Do you more often rely upon your own strength or His?
2. How does it feel when the Lord holds you during your storms?
3. How would you describe your personal feeling of being brave?
4. How difficult is it for you to express need to others? To God?

3 | Jump!

September 10, 2015

Reagan loves to jump! She even jumps when she is walking and holding my hand. There is something about lifting her feet up in the air and then coming back down that excites her. So when it came time to take that first leap into the pool, at the ripe old age of nineteen months, she was all in—literally! There was no need for coaxing or bribing. There was nothing except one word: "Jump!"

Splash!

"Let's do it again, Nana!" she exclaimed again and again.

When she jumped into the pool, she knew I would be there to catch her. A few times, her head went a little farther under the water than she would have preferred, but she understood that I would always be ready to take care of her. She totally relied upon me because she trusted me.

I once read a quote that was next to a picture of a person jumping off a cliff. It said something like, "Sometimes you just have to grow wings going down." It must have been a poster about courage or trust. And that is what Reagan displayed when she jumped into the water and my arms. Her courage grew because of her trust.

I hope and pray that my little spitfire granddaughter will

exude that same kind of courage and trust throughout her life. There is no reason why she shouldn't jump because her provider and her protector is the Lord, God Almighty! She need not fear because she can trust Him. I pray that we can all learn from her unwavering example of jumping. We can absolutely trust that in all situations, our sovereign Lord's open arms are there to hold us and to never let us sink. *Never.*

Key Thought

Jump!

Scripture

"Trust in the LORD with all your heart and lean not on your own understanding" (Proverbs 3:5).

Prayer

Thank You, Lord, for being our rescuer and our protector. Thank You that we can trust You, and that gives us courage. Thank You for the excitement of knowing that we can grow wings when we jump because You are faithful. If we falter, help us to remember that You are the solid rock that stabilizes us, holds us, and enables us to jump! Thank You for Your loving arms that are always ready to catch us and to hold us. In Christ's name we pray. Amen.

For Further Reflection

1. What kinds of circumstances cause you to pause even though you know you should jump?

2. Are there people in your life whom you trust and have been empowered by? Name them.
3. Describe some situations you have overcome and why you no longer shrink back.
4. Describe a time when you literally felt the Lord's intervention that enabled you to jump. Thank Him now.

"Courage is fear that has said its prayers."

—Eleanor Doan[1]

4 | Tank Coo, God!

September 10, 2015

A few months ago, Reagan and I were blessed to see a stunningly beautiful rainbow that lasted about thirty minutes. Sometimes it was a double rainbow, and most of the time, it was in complete form from one end to the other. It was amazing! While we were standing outside on the sidewalk watching the awesome display, a neighbor drove up in her car, stopped, and asked us, "How can anyone question whether there is a God or not? Look at the sky!"

Reagan had never seen a rainbow before, and she was very excited. She kept pointing up at the sky in amazement. As we were looking at the incredible display, I explained to her that God made the rainbow and we should say thank you to Him for the beauty He created for us. Without any hesitation, she immediately responded, "Tank Coo, God!"

We have not seen another rainbow, but every single time we walk outside, Reagan points up to the area of the sky where we saw the spectacular rainbow, and she ever so sweetly says, "Tank Coo, God!" Even though she can't see the rainbow anymore, she still remembers.

There is a big lesson to be learned here. Our Creator blesses us with marvelous gifts all the time, but do we remember to thank Him? When was the last time we said "thank You" for a rainbow and the beautiful message it represents? Reagan has not even been told the story yet, but she already knows to say, "Tank Coo, God!" May we all follow her lead.

Key Thought

Always remember to say thank You to God.

Scripture

"From the lips of children and infants, You have ordained praise" (Psalm 8:2).

Prayer

Thank You, Lord, for being the Creator of all things. Thank You, Lord, for rainbows and Your promise to never flood the earth again. Thank You, Lord, for the sweet innocence and spontaneity of children. May we always remember to express our gratitude to You not only for rainbows but for all things great and small. In Your Holy name we pray. Amen.

For Further Reflection

1. What circumstances cause you to immediately respond with words of praise?
2. What are some things or people that you take for granted and rarely remember to offer words of gratitude?
3. Is it easy, effortless, difficult, or somewhere in between for you to say "thank you"?

4. Is there a difference between gratitude and thankfulness? Explain.

> **"Gratitude is not only the greatest of virtues but the parent of all others."**
>
> —Marcus Tullius Cicero

> **"Gratitude turns what we have into enough."**
>
> —Anonymous

5 | Push, Push, Push ...

September 19, 2015

When Reagan was born, she was pushed in a stroller that epitomized comfort. We had a top-of-the-line baby carriage for our precious little girl! Now that she is a little older, that deluxe stroller is not quite as attractive, primarily because it is so heavy. Consequently, after some serious deliberation, we decided to buy an umbrella stroller. What a big difference! It is much lighter, and it collapses easily. Whew!

The one thing that we did not count on was that Reagan would want to push it, not ride in it! Yikes! More often than not, she insists that she wants to push, push, push with all of her twenty-six pounds of might and never relinquish control of the handles, whether she is going uphill or downhill. Nope! Reagan is the handler, whether she can accomplish it or not. And truth be told, it is way too much for her, especially when going up these hills in Colorado Springs, where the air is thin.

On this particular day, Reagan would have nothing to do with accepting help. When offered, she very humorlessly replied, "No, Nana, I want to do it myself!"

As we crept at a snail's pace going uphill, it became obvious that changing the direction would be extremely helpful. We could turn around and go downhill, and she could still push. It was a tactic designed to solve this struggle another way since her determination to continue pushing would not be compromised. So in a somewhat sly way, we managed to turn around and continue our journey much more easily downhill.

There are many of us who do exactly the same thing. We don't have the wisdom to recognize that some of those proverbial hills are just too hard to climb. Often we lack the humility to stop when we know we have reached our limit. God is there to help us, but we stubbornly say, "No!" The pride factor looms large. We do not want to relinquish our control to His wisdom.

On the other hand, if we don't try, we will never know if we could have made it. Tenacity and determination are wonderful when tempered with common sense. Lofty goals are admirable. However, the "I want to do it myself" mentality can get us into big trouble. If we would just have the wisdom to remember that our Lord is traversing all those hills with us, His grace would guide our journey.

A big part of me admired the way Reagan pushed and struggled to retain her control of that stroller. As she grows each day, she will become a little stronger and a little bigger, and then it will not be so hard for her to make it all the way up the hill. I just pray that as she grows physically, she will also grow in wisdom.

May we all wish for that same kind of ability to make good decisions, knowing what is and is not realistic. May we have the wisdom to seek the Lord's counsel in all situations. Every single time I witness Reagan's determination though, I thank God for her desire to push. I hope that Reagan will never lose her grip on that. Guided by the light the Lord provides, may we all embrace the desire to push, push, push!

Key Thought

Determination is good when the goal is realistic.

Scripture

"Do not be wise in your own eyes; fear the LORD and shun evil" (Proverbs 3:7).

Serenity Prayer

God grant me the serenity to accept the things I cannot change, courage to change the things I can, and the wisdom to know the difference. In Christ's holy name we pray. Amen (Reinhold Niebuhr).

For Further Reflection

1. When have you pushed too hard and the outcome was not good?
2. What lessons have you learned from pushing too hard?
3. Are you able to identify people in your life who help you to maintain balance in your life?
4. What are some of the characteristics of people who demonstrate the wisdom to know when to push and when to let go?

6 | But Where are the Reindeer?

December 15, 2015

One of the most enjoyable things that my husband I were able to do this Christmas season was to take Reagan to see Santa Claus. We were so happy to see her walk right up to the jolly old fellow and sit on his lap. When asked what she wanted for Christmas, at the ripe old age of two, that question was just too hard to answer. She stared at him with a very puzzled face. He then handed her a dolly, and she was on her way.

As we sat and watched the other children walk up to Santa, it was apparent that something really bothered Reagan. She looked at me very seriously, and her lip was just about to quiver when she asked, "But where are the reindeer, Nana? Where are the reindeer?"

Only Santa could answer a question like that. So together we marched right back up to him and asked, "Where are the reindeer?"

He appeared to be as befuddled as Reagan by that inquiry! So I ever so gently asked Santa if he left the reindeer up on the roof. I could see him thinking, *Ah, yes! That's where the reindeer are. Up on the roof!* With the problem solved, Reagan pranced away to get a cookie.

When things don't add up, we can either pursue finding out

the answer or let go of the issue. Reagan was not about to let her question go unanswered. After all, knowing the whereabouts of Santa's reindeer was a very important question that needed an answer.

Some questions to extrapolate from this experience might include the following: What issues do we leave unanswered that we shouldn't? Are the reasons valid that stop us from pursuing the answers? What kinds of ideas, fascinations, or preoccupations serve to appease us?

We all respond in different ways to those queries, and the degree to which we avoid or pursue our questions says a lot about us. As we continue to search, the Lord promises to be our constant Companion during our quest. Proverbs 2:6 reminds us, "The LORD gives wisdom and from His mouth comes knowledge and understanding." We need to commit to keep seeking His guidance whether to pursue challenging questions or not. The Lord is not Santa Claus, and He does not need any coaxing for answers. His timing is perfect, and He will provide enough light for our understanding. Our Savior and guide is always with us, and He is forever faithful to help us know how to resolve our every need.

Key Thought

God is faithful as we seek.

Scripture

"For the LORD gives wisdom and from His mouth come knowledge and understanding" (Proverbs 2:6).

Prayer

Heavenly Lord, You supply all of our needs, and You are faithful to be our guide, our guard, and our shield. We humbly ask You to help us to never stop searching and to be always listening for Your voice. Please give us ears to hear. Thank You for the lesson from my precious, inquisitive granddaughter. When the questions are harder, please help us to know Your will on how best to resolve our uncertainties. Thank You that You are our sovereign Lord. In Christ's name, we pray. Amen.

For Further Reflection

1. Is it your natural inclination to go to the Lord first for answers or to seek the counsel of others?
2. Have you ever questioned God's faithfulness? If so, what was the result?
3. We all know waiting for answers is difficult. What keeps you vigilant? If you have been unsuccessful while waiting, how have you pursued getting back on track?
4. How do you deal with impatience when you think you need an answer right away?

7 | Good Job, Nana!

June 13, 2016

I find it interesting that when little children want to do something, they usually have amazing persistence. Often that unrelenting resolve proves successful! Such was the case during a recent walk with Reagan. She loves pushing her stroller, and even though the handles are taller than her head, with outstretched arms, she tenaciously pushes. On this hot, eighty-nine-degree afternoon, Reagan decided that she wanted to push the stroller all the way around my very large neighborhood block. I explained to her that the hills were very hard to go up, but to no avail. With all her twenty-nine pounds of might, she showed no signs of wanting to yield to the heat or to the hills.

Truth be told, I was hot, and I did not want to walk up and down those hills. But Reagan insisted and proceeded to explain that she was going on a trip. I relented, and we slowly trudged ahead. Along the way, we learned about shade. We both agreed that it was okay to take a little break under the shade of a tree, which was near the sidewalk. We both enjoyed that.

About twenty minutes after we had our conversation about hills, Reagan said to me, "Good job, Nana!" Wow! My heart swelled to think that she was commending me on my good job as she kept pushing the stroller up the hill. I replied that she was doing a good job too. She breathlessly answered, "Thank you" as we continued our trek. The fact that she was thinking about me took my already short breath away!

My thoughts were all about finishing that walk, but Reagan's thoughts were about thanking me! Good job, Reagan!

Key Thought

Thanking, even when it is hard and you are walking up hills, matters.

Scripture

"From the lips of children and infants, You have ordained praise" (Matthew 21:16).

Prayer

Thank You, Lord, for the words of praise from my granddaughter today. What a lesson I learned during that uphill walk! Reagan was the one doing all the work, and she was the one thinking about me! Thank You for the hills, the shade, and the lesson learned on our trip. Thank You for Your presence with us at all times. To God be the glory. Amen.

For Further Reflection

1. As you travail on your trail, do you remember to offer words of gratitude?
2. How do you respond when others thank you?
3. Is it difficult or easy for you to receive words of praise? Give reasons for your answer.
4. When was the last time you thanked the Lord for your life?

Two Little Hands in Mine

Rachel Denison, my mother

As I stroll through the orchard with two little hands in mine,
I feel the scented breezes and the caress of soft sunshine—

Sprinkling through the apple blossoms on this glorious
day, as the birds sing sweetly welcoming May!

I feel the gentle softness of these innocent hands, and I
point to the wonder of nature which around us expands;

"See the birds, see the trees, see the wildflowers—what
beauty has been made by the long Spring showers!"

The hands break away and run to pick a bloom
from a nearby posy in the orchard's room.

Retracing my footsteps with senses refined, I pray that
these small hands will be for goodness inclined!

8 | I Can't Stop!

June 14, 2016

Our night out to eat at the bowling alley was delicious for my spirit. My husband and I ordered a grilled cheese sandwich for our granddaughter, Reagan. When an adult, super-sized sandwich arrived, dripping with ooey-gooey cheddar cheese, Reagan immediately started chomping away. Yum! About two-thirds through, however, she looked at us and grimly said, "My tummy hurts." We assured her that she did not have to finish that huge sandwich.

She then promptly replied, "But I can't stop!"

We laughed. How cute! And how true! We all do the same thing, don't we? We take one spoon from the half-gallon ice cream container and then another and another until we are in a sugar stupor and asking ourselves why we ate so much.

It is not just food either. It may be clothes, money, or even exercise. You name it! We all too often have a hard time stopping. No one taught us to be gluttonous. It just seems to be in our DNA to think that more is better, and besides, that gooey cheese tastes so yummy. What's the harm?

Our dinner at the bowling alley taught me a lesson. Instead of laughing, I could have easily suggested that we take the rest of the sandwich home to eat later and then there would be no hurting tummy. I still think her response was totally adorable, but the next time when I am pressing my own limits eating french fries, I am going to remind myself that I can stop. And I will. Learning self-control is tough. But I can help Reagan now, and she can begin to learn that stopping can be a good thing.

Key Thought

Just because it tastes good does not mean that it is good for you.

Scripture

"So then, let us not be like the others, who are asleep, but let us be alert and self-controlled" (1 Timothy 5:6).

Prayer

Dear heavenly Lord, You offer us such an abundance of blessings that we so enjoy! Thank You for all these wonderful gifts. Please, Lord, help us to be self-controlled in our taking, and most importantly, help us to remember that nothing can quench our desires but Your Holy Spirit. Thank You for truly being our all in all. May we never be lured by anything less. With grateful hearts, we pray in Christ's name. Amen.

For Further Reflection

1. In what areas of your life do you tend to overindulge?
2. What is your response to your indulgences? Shame? Guilt? Acceptance? Justification?

3. If possible, name an area of your life that you will commit to getting under better control and list specific ways you intend to do so.

4. Do you believe that God is able and willing to help you with self-restraint? Explain your reasoning.

9 | Now You Are Sad, Nana

December 16, 2016

My husband and I have the good fortune of having Reagan with us almost every week. We usually pick her up from daycare around four o'clock on Fridays, and the fun begins from the moment we see each other. She drops whatever she is doing and runs excitedly to us. She jumps in our arms, and for the next twenty-four hours, all of us— Nana, Bampa, and Reagan—are in "Bliss Land."

It does not matter what Reagan does or does not do. We think everything is brilliant and adorable. We play, laugh, and say yes to *almost* all the things she wants to do. After all, that is what grandparents do best! With the sweetest granddaughter in the whole world, the choice is easy! Reagan recently requested ice cream for breakfast. We all agreed that was a wonderful idea! Yum!

We delight in a very meaningful ritual of doing three-way hugs. I stand on the first step of the stairs, and Bampa holds Reagan while standing at the foot of the stairs. That way we are all on the same level with each other. We then all hug and kiss each other. This always happens before we say goodnight, when we greet each other, and many, many times in between.

We are eye to eye with one another, and it is very important to each of us.

When it is time to part ways, Reagan always says, "Now you are going to be sad, Nana, because I am leaving." She then goes on to explain to me that I will be happy when I see her again, but then her mommy will be sad because she has left her. She is very sympathetic about my sadness and often offers to kiss me again before she leaves to go with Mommy. Reagan is also very aware that whomever she is with, she is loved. She knows that loving her makes us all happy.

The lesson here is pretty straightforward. It is a joyful experience to love someone. To have a sympathetic heart toward someone who is sad is a compassionate act of love. It is so simple, and yet we often struggle with those feelings. And it then becomes complicated. Now that is what is sad.

I pray that our tender feelings toward each other will grow and remain pure and uncomplicated. It is so easy to love Reagan. If only we could keep it that simple with others: love one another.

Key Thought

Loving brings joy.

Scripture

"Your love has given me great joy and encouragement because your brother has refreshed the hearts of the saints" (Philemon 1:7).

Prayer

Thank You, Lord, for the pure joy of loving my granddaughter so much and for the lessons I learn from her. Help me to have a heart to share that love as easily with others whom I encounter. Thank You for Your everlasting and abundant love. In Christ's name, we pray. Amen.

For Further Reflection

1. How often do you express words of love to God, your family, and your friends?
2. Expressing words of affection as well as receiving them is difficult for many people. How about you?
3. Do you think your conduct reflects the fact that God loves you? How?
4. Are you struggling with your feelings about love? If so, how are you addressing that issue?

10 | Really?!

February 23, 2017

We had not seen our precious Reagan for over three weeks, and we could hardly wait to see her excited, sparkling eyes and feel the rush of her embrace. As was our usual routine, we went to her classroom at daycare to pick her up at the appointed hour. She saw us, immediately dropped her toy, and started to run toward us! Yes! Our adorable little one was on her way to us until the teacher said in a stern, raised voice, "Stop, Reagan!"

What! No! This can't be! You mean teacher, you just squelched our much-anticipated reunion moment! Really? Ugh! With all the self-control I could muster, I thought those thoughts but did not say them. Now days later, I am still thinking about it though.

Reagan was then instructed to put away her toy properly and to walk to us, not run. Obediently she did as she was told and then came to us, but her spirit was a bit depleted. The teacher told us that she had to be consistent with her rules: no running and put toys away correctly. My heart still hurts that Reagan looked so wounded when she was reprimanded. She had been so exuberant just seconds before.

I reluctantly concede that consistency matters. I also freely admit that Reagan got over the incident faster than I did. I am still wondering if it would have been so horrible for an exception to be made. After all, the teacher knew we had not seen Reagan in a long while. Is there a right or a wrong answer here?

For the sake of trying to develop a takeaway from this scenario, I will, however, somewhat reluctantly yield to the teacher. Lots of other kids were in the room, and if one kid drops a toy and runs, then I suppose it sends the message that it is okay for everyone to do so. It is hard to be obedient, especially when there are gray areas like this one and a child's and grandparent's hearts are so vulnerable and tender.

Jesus feels our pain, knows our sorrows, and bears our burdens with us. Knowingly and unknowingly, we daily hurt each other. When Jesus walked this earth, He was spat upon and grievously wounded for our transgressions. And He never stopped loving us. He was consistent and steadfastly pursued His mission to love us, even to death on the cross.

From a preschool classroom to the cross is a whopping leap, I know. But that is the lesson I choose to draw from this event. Reagan was obedient to her teacher. Her shoulders drooped, and the spring in her step disappeared, but she listened and obeyed. Again, she got over her disappointment faster than Bampa and I did.

Overcoming difficulties can be very problematic for all of us. Sometimes it seems that the older we are, the harder it gets! That is especially true when we lose our focus on what really matters. The single most important thing to remember is that God is our guide in all situations. Keeping our eyes on the cross empowers us, and obedience to authority can become less burdensome. I remember reading once that submission requires an inner strength to obey God.

Yes, I know that Reagan's teacher had all authority in the classroom. Reagan got past the incident quickly, and it is probably not even in her memory. My writing this today is helping me to let go, and it is reminding me that holding on to hurts shifts my attention needlessly.

May the lesson from the preschool classroom extend beyond the boundaries of that moment!

Key Thought

Yield to authority.

Scripture

"Obey your leaders and submit to their authority. They keep watch over you as men who must give an account. Obey them so that their work will be a joy and not a burden, for that would be of no advantage to you" (Hebrews 13:17).

Prayer

Dear Lord, please forgive us for getting so caught up in everyday exchanges that we allow them to shift our eyes away from You. Help us to be obedient to Your will and Your direction. May we willingly yield to those who have authority over us. Please help us to be obedient to Your Word. Thank You, Lord Jesus. Amen.

For Further Reflection

1. Do you have difficulty submitting to authority? Explain.
2. What do you think are some reasons why being obedient is so challenging?
3. Does pride make yielding to authority harder? If so, how?
4. Are you able to think of an example when obedience has been a joyful act? Explain.

11 | Actually …

Words make a difference, and there are times when one word can make a huge difference. The word today and the subject of this meditation is "actually." Numerous times in the past twenty-four hours as I have had the pleasure to be with Reagan, she has given me an answer, thought about it, and then revised her reply with, "Actually that is not quite right." Then she proceeded to correct her response. Wow! She is three and a half years old, and she is thinking so very conscientiously about her reply! That we would all do the same with our responses!

So often we say something awkwardly and don't take the time to correct our statements. We let the moment pass and make up a variety of excuses for failing to explain what we really meant to say and cavalierly think it was not that important to clarify. Too often, that is flawed thinking. People and words matter. Most of us were taught to think before we speak. How often do we?

There is a difference between spoken words and God's written Word. Our sovereign Lord inspired the written Word, and He chose His words and the men who wrote them very carefully. It seems appropriate to me to glean His guidance from the passage from Psalm 119:130 that says, "The unfolding of your words gives light; it gives understanding to the simple."

How do words give understanding to the simple? For my

interpretation, it appears from this verse that we are being encouraged to expand our explanations, even when the subject may be simple. When we have an inkling that we haven't used the correct words, we need to listen to our inner voice. "Actually" is the transition word that conveys, "I am giving this more thought, I care about completing this conversation the right way, and I care about you. So I will take the time to answer more thoroughly."

Reagan's sweet, deliberate response is now planted in my heart, and although she might not know the difference now when I respond to her, I know the difference. And actually, whether she is three or thirty-three, I will endeavor to always thoughtfully reply to her with words that will give her light.

Key Thought

Words matter.

Scripture

"Your statutes are wonderful; therefore, I obey them. The unfolding of your words gives light; it gives understanding to the simple" (Psalm 119:130).

Prayer

Heavenly Lord, thank You for Your words. May we hear them and heed them. May our conversations be glorifying to You. When we feel that our words have been incorrect, insufficient, or dishonoring, implant in us the commitment to respond appropriately. Thank You for Your words of truth and light and for this lesson from my dear granddaughter. In Your holy name, I pray. Amen.

For Further Reflection

1. How careful are you with your words?
2. How often do you amend your reply when you know your response has been inadequate?
3. Do you think everyone deserves such attention to detail?
4. How important is it to you that you use the correct word that accurately reflects your intentions?

12 | Broken Hearts Do Mend

March 25, 2017

Many years ago, I heard a testimonial by Damaris Cárbaugh, one of my very favorite Christian singers. She explained that she was at very low point in her life and that she wanted to give her heart to God but her heart was broken. How could she give her heart away when her heart was broken? She then realized that she just needed to give what she had—her broken heart.

When we feel deficient and think we have nothing to give, we are often the most vulnerable, the neediest, and often the most receptive. In the depths of our despair, we feel hopeless, and there is little, if anything, that will console us. But in the darkest hour, the light is brightest.

These are the thoughts that came to me when my dear three-and-a-half-year-old Reagan told me with such deep distress and seriousness, "Mommy broke my heart today." With all the sympathy an adoring Nana could provide, I exclaimed, "Oh no! That's terrible. What happened?" Then there was a very long pause, and she thoughtfully said, "I don't know."

Actually she didn't remember. The memory of the hurt was still there, but a happy time at daycare erased the exact detail of the pain, and now, of course, she was with her Nana.

For adults, it is not that easy to let go of things that cause us to feel hurt and broken. Our hearts carry burdens for which only God can provide comfort and healing. His sovereignty over all our joys and sorrows is much too vast for us to understand. Of course, we might try, but that ends up being unproductive. We will never understand, but we can know that He wants our hearts, broken as they are, just the way they are.

What a true comfort it is to know that we don't have to try to do the mending. Our Master Healer is with us to provide what we need in our time of need. And that is precisely what happened today. Reagan's comment about her broken heart was a prompt to remind me that only the healer of our hearts can make us whole.

Key Thought

The Lord is the healer of our hearts.

Scripture

"The sacrifices of God are a broken spirit, a broken and contrite heart" (Psalm 51:17).

Prayer

Dear Lord, Thank You for loving us, broken as we are. Thank You for knowing us, inside and out. As the psalmist asks, please "restore unto me the joy of Thy salvation and grant me a willing spirit to sustain me." Help us, Lord, to not foolishly try to hide from You or ourselves. May our hearts feel Your power and Your healing as we yield them to You. We praise You for who You are! In Your great name, we pray. Amen.

For Further Reflection

1. Letting go of hurts is very hard to do. What has been your experience?
2. Provide words for what a broken heart feels like.
3. Do you really believe it is possible to totally forgive when a grievous assault has occurred?
4. What are some practical ways you yield your hurts to Jesus?

13 | "You Just Have to Wait, Nana"

April 3, 2017

Every time I am going to be away from Reagan for more than a week, I am genuinely sad. She is a bright light that I look forward to experiencing each time we are together, and my heart is happier because I am with her. So when I drove Reagan and her mom to a motel in Denver the night before they needed to board a very early airplane flight, I was feeling sorry that she would be gone. When it was time to say our goodbyes, I told Reagan that I would miss her, I was sad to see her leave, and I wished I could go with her. I was sitting on the side of the bed in the motel as I was saying these things to her. She immediately came to be by my side and sat next to me. She put her little arm around me and started gently patting my back and shoulder. With all the compassion she had in her entire being, she sweetly said, "Nana, you can't go this time. You'll just have to wait, Nana. It's okay, Nana. It's okay."

Her tenderness and loving voice were so compassionate and heartfelt that I practically melted down through the floor. She cared so deeply about my being okay while she was away. Her little hand on my shoulder seemed to envelope my entire body, not just my shoulder. Her heart was so totally focused on comforting my heart.

Our heavenly Father is our comforter, our healer of wounded hearts, and the lover of our souls. He knows our pain, and He is always with us. But sometimes we don't feel His arms. That is not because He is not there. And it is not because He is not holding us. Mostly I think it is because we either don't know how or we don't willingly yield our hurting hearts to Him.

When I was with Reagan, I really did not want to see her go. In a way, I wanted to hold on to my sadness, but then I knew I would tell myself to "buck up." I do miss her, but mostly now, I am hoping that she will have a great time while she is away. And I can hardly wait to hear about her adventures. I must patiently wait.

Waiting is hard. But it is less difficult when our Savior is waiting in the wings with us. It is also less grim when we yield to His embrace and let go of our expectations of ourselves and have faith in Him. We can't second-guess God. If He has chosen for us to wait, we can choose to submit to His timing and have the absolute assurance that we are not alone.

I have decided to believe that Reagan's little hand on me and her telling me that I needed to wait was directly sent from heaven through her to me. That is more than just okay. That is God!

Key Thought

We are not alone when we wait.

Scripture

"Yet the Lord longs to be gracious to you; he rises to show you compassion. For the Lord is a God of justice. Blessed are all who wait for Him" (Isaiah 30:18).

Prayer

Thank You, Lord, for the myriad of marvelous ways You choose to reveal Your divine presence. Thank You for touching our hearts in so many different ways. Thank You for my feeling Your touch through my granddaughter's hand. Help us to trust You as we wait. Thank You that we have the assurance that You are always with us, even when we are waiting on You. In Your Name we pray. Amen.

For Further Reflection

1. What has been your experience when you have had to wait upon the Lord?
2. How have you felt the Lord use others to make His presence known to you?
3. Do you battle with impatience? If so, what have you learned during your struggle?
4. Has the Lord used you to comfort others during their waiting time? If so, how?

14 | Oh Boy! Oh Boy!! Oh Boy!!!

April 10, 2017

There is a beautiful contemporary song entitled "I Can Only Imagine" that basically asks the question, "How will I react when I see Jesus?" Trying to imagine the moment, the lyrics offer scenarios such as, "Will I stand in silence and in awe be still or will I sing Hallelujah, or be able to speak at all?" I wonder how many of us have thoughtfully tried to envision how we would react. Of course, we will only know when we have the glorious blessing of meeting Christ face-to-face. That first encounter is truly something to think about and to be really, really, really excited about!

Firsts are special. We remember our first love, our first kiss, our first real loss ... and the list goes on. A trip to the mountains, specifically up to the entrance of the Cave of the Winds Mountain Park in Manitou Springs, Colorado, was a first for Reagan. This amazing attraction is in the foothills of the Rocky Mountains, and the drive up to the cave is spectacular. The scenery as you climb up the hill is stunningly beautiful. The red rocks and the views take your breath away. Literally, Reagan breathlessly and excitedly exclaimed, "Oh boy! Oh boy! Oh boy!" as we climbed higher and higher up the mountain in our car. The pitch of her enthusiasm rose as we ascended.

As I took great pleasure in observing her absolute thrill, I was aware that my desire to feel that overjoyed about something— anything—was sparked. Hmm. When was the last time I was that excited? How contagious was her glee! What a catalyst it was for me! How very exhilarating it was to experience her total ecstasy! Then the aha moment came when I realized that I was also breathlessly experiencing her jubilant elation! Oh boy! Oh boy! Oh boy! Thank You, God!

Many of my firsts were a long time ago. I have enjoyed many wonderful experiences, and I know that I am truly spoiled. My been-there-done-that mentality most definitely needs correcting. Everyday marvelous wonders like sunrises, sunsets, snow falling, and green grass are all extraordinary miracles that deserve wide-open eyes as well as wide-open spirits. A myriad of colors, sounds, and thoughts are waiting to be savored, explored, and appreciated every single day.

The opportunity to be refreshed and renewed is available to us at all times if only we would choose to avail ourselves to the wellspring of life, our Savior Jesus Christ. Cultivating a thankful heart is the way that we can do that. How wonderful it would be if we could all wake up each day exclaiming, "Oh boy! Oh boy!! Oh boy!!!"

Key Thought

Always be open to wonder.

Scripture

"I will extol the LORD at all times, His praise will always be on my lips" (Psalm 34:1).

Prayer

Thank You, Lord, that our little excursion to the mountains proved to be a mountaintop experience for me. Help me to remember that You are sovereign over all things and Creator of them all. Thank You for the majesty of Your universe and help us all to give You the glory unceasingly for all Your mighty works. Thank You for the powerful reminder of Your greatness through the beauty of nature and the exclamations of a child. Lord, please help us to be open to the wonder of it all. In the name of Jesus Christ, we pray. Amen.

For Further Reflection

1. Do you remember the last time you exclaimed shouts of wonder?
2. When was the last time you offered words of gratitude for the everyday things you might take for granted?
3. Describe a mountaintop moment and share your experience.
4. Spend time with the Lord, thanking Him for things that you don't usually mention.

15 | Seeing the Forest and the Trees

May 12, 2017

Recently Reagan and I were looking out the upstairs window at my house. I don't remember exactly what we were trying to see. But what I do recall was her comment, "Look, Nana, we are level with the trees." Her awareness of her surroundings and her astute observation took me by surprise. She knew where she was, what she saw, and what she was looking for. How could a three-and-a-half-year-old be that focused and articulate?

Later that day, Reagan and her mom were playing with a balloon. They were having a great time batting the balloon back and forth in my living room. Her mom was sitting on a chair, and Reagan was standing. That's when I heard from Mommy, "You see, Reagan, we are level with each other so it is easier to pass the balloon back and forth." There was that word, "level," again.

This discourse made me start thinking about how we get so ensnared in our thoughts, ideas, or circumstances that we often limit our perspective and our possibilities. Being aware of our surroundings helps us to enjoy expanded thinking. Reagan was keenly interested in all that was within her purview. That realization prompted another memory for me.

Years ago, when I was teaching a humanities class, several

young college students were commenting that they were either too stressed, tired, preoccupied, or apathetic to look at the scenery in our beautiful town. As they drove their cars to and from their destinations, they were not at all interested in looking beyond the road. I was stunned. After all, Pike's Peak, the mountain that inspired the writing of "America the Beautiful," is right here!

They explicitly stated that they were totally disinterested in looking at the mountains as they drove past them on the interstate each morning. How sad! A simple turn of the head to the right as they went south or a glance to the left as they went north might have made a difference in their day. Beauty is everywhere if we just choose to see it and connect with it.

I pray that Reagan will always be aware of her surroundings and that it will be personal for her. It may be to bat at a balloon or to gaze at a mountain. Whatever the circumstance, it will most assuredly add beauty and perspective to her day.

Key Thought

It is possible to see the forest and the trees, and that is what keeps us level.

Scripture

"I lift up mine eyes to the hills—where does my help come from? My help comes from the LORD, the Maker of heaven and earth" (Psalm 121:1–2).

Prayer

Heavenly Lord, whether in the depths of despair or on the mountaintop shouting for joy, You are there. Evidence of Your presence is everywhere. Please help us to keep our eyes wide open and help us to be aware so we can experience the wonder You have in store for us. You are the master leveler, and we praise You for Your awesome works in us and around us. In Your mighty name we pray. Amen.

For Further Reflection

1. How often do you intentionally look to try to grasp all you can see?
2. Do you sometimes find yourself lost in the forest? If so, how do you find your way out?
3. Is it important for you to experience beauty? Why or why not?
4. How do you acknowledge the presence of the Lord in your everyday routine?

16 | Polka-Dot Pizza

May 28, 2017

Sometimes there are encounters so precious that you never ever forget them. And the trigger that the memory is associated with is forever personalized in your mind and heart. From now on, every single time I see a pepperoni pizza, I will think of Reagan's delightful explanation of it.

Reagan was telling me that there was a "Donimos" (Yes, it is spelled correctly!) right next to her daycare center and that she and Mommy just went there to eat. When I asked her what she had, she very thoughtfully told me that it was round and red and it had polka dots! Is that adorable or what? Yep, from now on, pepperoni pizza is now permanently renamed "polka-dot pizza"!

That sweet exchange reminded me of another recollection that I have enjoyed for more than fifty years. Every spring, my parents would take my sisters and me to Georgia to see our sweet Aunt Bitsy. It was a long car ride from New Jersey, and with great anticipation, we looked forward to being with her. During one of our visits, she repeatedly told us about a wonderful new ice cream place that was about ten miles from her house. We were extremely happy about going there, but with the way Aunt Bitsy drove, it took an enormously long time. If her shiny, little gray Lancer car *ever* went *over* twenty-five miles an hour, I was never fortunate enough to have been the passenger. Oh well, the ice cream was supposed to be wonderful, and Aunt Bitsy was so looking forward to taking us that even if we were just going to eat ice cubes, it would not matter. We were with Aunt Bitsy!

So when we finally arrived at the much talked about ice cream place, we saw that it was a Dairy Queen. Really? Dairy Queen? Those places were all over New Jersey, and that was nothing new or special for us city girls. Yet because of Aunt Bitsy's thrill about taking us to a place that was really terrific in her eyes, we enjoyed our chocolate swirl cones like never before. And still, every single time I see a Dairy Queen, I think about my sweet Aunt Bitsy.

So often, it is not the thing that is important. Rather it is the memory associated with that thing. It is nice to enjoy chocolate swirl ice cream and pepperoni pizza, but it is even better to savor the memory of a dear loved one who made the treat even more special.

We can look at our beautiful Pike's Peak here in Colorado Springs and think what a beautiful mountain it is and leave it at that. Or we can see it as a majestic handprint of our Creator God. What a treat for our eyes! We know that everything in nature is a gift from God and there are incalculable amounts of exquisite examples of His extravagance everywhere. It behooves believers to acknowledge and give glory to the Maker of heaven and earth. When we do, our hearts and perspectives are forever changed.

After all, it is the heart that we remember that is associated with the mountain, the ice cream, and the polka-dot pizza. Wouldn't it be wonderful if we could view all things as God's treats for us?

Key Thought

Hearts shape what we see.

Scripture

"Great are the works of the LORD. They are pondered by all who delight in them" (Psalm 111:2).

Prayer

Dear heavenly Lord, Creator, and Maker of all things, how precious are the memories of dear loved ones whose hearts and words color the world. Thank You for memories that serve to make our lives so rich. It is out of Your abundance that we can enjoy all things great and small. May our eyes and ears be open to receive all that You have so generously lavished upon us. With grateful hearts, we give You praise. In Christ's name we pray. Amen.

For Further Reflection

1. Do you have a polka-dot pizza recollection? Share it.
2. How do you cultivate a grateful heart?
3. Do you have an Aunt Bitsy? Stop and thank God for the people who bless your life. Give God the glory for those people.
4. Thank the Lord for all the things that you feel are treats from God designed just for you.

17 | Choices

September 12, 2017

Making good choices is a lifelong pursuit. Very unfortunately, Reagan recently decided to cut herself off from being social when she is with adults who know and love her. She is aware and has been repeatedly informed that when she makes this decision, she is with friends and there is no stranger danger. Yet she hangs her head, clings to her mom's leg, and ignores all attempts of others to elicit a response. What a disappointing choice she has made.

As a hypervigilant Nana, her deliberate resolve to withdraw quite disturbs me. I want the whole world to know and love my brilliant, beautiful, and most extraordinary granddaughter. It might be too early to be worrying about our dear yet-to-be four-year-old, but I can't help it! I know her. I love her.

I wonder how the Lord must feel when we choose to be less than our best. The choice is ours to make. Sometimes we do it deliberately, and other times, we just allow ourselves to get into a rut without really thinking about it. What does it matter anyway? We tend to justify our thoughts that falsely appease that guilt that might try to slip in to awaken our apathy.

Recently Reagan and I were driving in the car to meet one of my friends, and on the way, she, in a very matter-of-fact way, declared, "I am going to be shy today." Another day, she informed me, "I am only going to say one thing." She had made her plans, and that was that.

Truth be told, all of us do the same thing to greater and lesser degrees. Sometimes we set boundaries appropriately. Other times, we do not. There are all kinds of reasons why we do not reach out to others when we could. How often do we yield to our lesser selves? How often do we do things that we know is not what the Lord would have us do, but after all, we are not really hurting anyone?

Well, actually, yes, we are. In Reagan's case, by limiting her contact with others, she is robbing us of the joy of knowing her more fully and therefore loving her more deeply. Hopefully, this is just a little kid phase that will pass. But I plan to intervene to support her development of social skills, and I am happy about that choice. Reagan and I are going to join a class together where we will enjoy the wonderful gift of music to free our spirits. Hopefully then Reagan will choose to beat a drum rather than cling to my leg.

We were all fearfully and wonderfully made with talents and gifts that are to be made known for the Lord's good purpose. This is a wake-up call for us to seek the Lord and to apply the insight that He promises to give us. Appropriately, Proverbs 20:11 reminds us, "even a child is known by his actions." Sometimes when we decide to remain silent, to not study His Word, to not His seek counsel, or to skip praying, we are making the same choice as Reagan's to be shy.

Let's choose to share and not withhold our gifts. Let's choose to honor our Lord and provider of abundance with all He has so generously lavished upon us. Let's choose not to be shy today!

Key Thought

You are blessed to be a blessing.

Scripture

"Blessings crown the head of the righteous" (Proverbs 10:6a).

Prayer

Thank You, Lord, that we are all so fearfully and wonderfully made. Thank You that we are blessed to be blessings for Your good purpose. Help us to stay in communion with You, to seek Your direction, and to glorify You in all things that bring honor to You. Thank You for the privilege to be able to explore the countless ways to bring glory to Your name. May our desire to know You and to do Your will grow forever. In Your holy name we pray. Amen.

For Further Reflection

1. Do you think that all the boundaries you have set are appropriate?
2. Has there ever been a time when you chose to be shy and the result was detrimental because of that decision?
3. How do you honor the Lord by your choices?
4. How do you bless others with your blessings?

"Hide not your talents, they for use were made. What's a sundial in the shade?"

—Benjamin Franklin

18 | Heart Flutters

September 21, 2017

Recently Reagan asked her mom if her dress looked pretty. Then she proceeded to say that she wanted to look nice for Luke.

"Luke?"

"Yes, he's a boy in my class, and I want to look pretty for him."

Reagan is starting out early on that quest for sure! It was cute and endearing to hear her then go on to explain about her new friend. But the conversation became even more adorable when she very simply stated, "He makes my heart flutter."

Heart flutter?

"Reagan, where did you hear that word?"

Reagan then very confidently replied, "It's just me."

Just hearing about this conversation between Reagan and her mom makes my heart flutter. And naturally, all that flapping inspired some deeper introspection. As I was thinking about just what it is that makes my heart flutter, I came up with an explanation that it is an excitement that can't be quelled. It is the feeling of a smile very deep inside that makes you feel happy, content, and joyful. It is in a category of its own. First loves can make hearts flutter. At the age of three years and eleven months,

I hope Reagan has experienced the first of multitudes of heart flutters.

Spiritually speaking, the feeling of the presence of the Holy Spirit makes one's heart flutter. It is a private and intimate experience, and only the person having it can appreciate its intricacies. The indwelling of the divine is something each person can enjoy, but it is not always as easy as it sounds. Our hearts often become guarded because of such things as hurts, disappointments, and sorrows. As we attempt to protect our broken or hurting hearts, we are prone to be less open to receive all the good that is waiting to enter. We frequently remind ourselves that when we are vulnerable, we can be hurt. Sadly we seem to listen to that voice too often. What about the voice that beckons us to receive all that the Lord has in store for us? How many of us even hear it, much less respond to it? Does life hand us so many obstacles and hardships that we yield more frequently to staying safe rather than choosing to be accessible?

It would be wonderful if we could unwaveringly decide to open our hearts to receive all that the Lord has for us. We would then have the blessed opportunity to realize that the tough things as well as the good things are all part of the grand design God has planned for us. Embracing that attitude and feeling the Lord's pleasure about that decision most certainly is a recipe for heart flutters.

Key Thought

Heart flutters are gifts to be enjoyed often.

Scripture

"Do not let your heart be troubled" (John 14:1).

Prayer

Thank You, Lord, for the fluttering hearts of both young and old. Thank You for Your promise to guide us and bless us. Thank You for Your Holy Spirit and for the flutter that renews our spirit. Help us to seek You and to remain wide open to receive all that You have ordained for us. With hearts full of gratitude, we praise Your holy name. Amen.

For Further Reflection

1. Describe what makes your heart flutter.
2. Have you experienced a Holy Spirit heart flutter? If so, please describe it.
3. Have you intentionally protected your heart because of hurts, sorrows, and pain? If so, do you think this has limited your opportunities to be open to heart flutters?
4. How often do you enjoy heart flutters?

19 | His Internet Is Never Down

September 26, 2017

It is so frustrating to me when the electronics in my house don't work. If the TV does not come on or when there are crackly sounds on the radio, I immediately get mad and too often say bad words. I absolutely have never understood how we actually manage to get all of this reception either. Whether it is cable or wireless, it is all very, very impressive to me. If we could see the radio waves and if Wi-Fi connections were visible, it would probably blow our minds. All the inner workings that it takes to keep this techy world functioning is truly amazing to me.

Reagan has grown up with computer tablet games and knew how to use the basic functions on the TV remote while she was enjoying her not-so-terrible twos. So I should not have been surprised by her remark when the TV came on but would not connect to any channels.

I was thinking, *Oh no! How will Reagan survive without the much-anticipated episode of the Mickey Mouse Club?* when she very accurately stated, "Oh, Nana, it is just the internet that is down." Not yet four years old, how in the world does she know about the internet?

I wonder how the Lord must feel when our internet is down.

He certainly does not get mad and say bad things! But I am sure His heart is sad that we are not open to receive Him. There are lots of reasons why our spirits may be down or even closed off. We are experts at listing all the reasons why we shut down communications.

Ironically, the way we might respond when we feel like the Lord is not hearing us is to actually turn on that TV and listen to things we shouldn't and even to say those bad things. We are very clever at devising all kinds of ways to escape. We may falsely try to convince ourselves that He isn't really listening anyway.

Encouragingly for me, Reagan is not only confident about her understanding of the internet, she also boldly displays certainty in her understanding about God loving and taking care of her. Despite the internet being down, her trust in the Lord is functioning very well. While we were trying to figure out how to get the internet back up, I asked her about an ouchy that I noticed on her hand. She quickly and confidently answered by assuring me, "It is going to be okay, Nana. God is fixing it right now."

As we grow and learn to navigate all the twists and turns and ups and downs of life, we would be wise to choose to keep our receptors turned on and tuned in to the one and only source who is the wellspring of life. After all, God is always tuned into us. His internet is never down. He is always available, and He hears us whether our spiritual cables are brand new or split and frayed.

Internet down? No problem. God can still hear me right now.

Key Thought

God's internet is never down.

Scripture

"He who has ears, let him hear" (Matthew 11:15).

Prayer

Thank You, dear heavenly Lord, for always being available. Help us to keep our ears attuned to hear Your voice. And when we don't hear You, help us to trust that we will. Thank You for the freedom to be heard, known, and loved by You. Thank You for Your omnipresence. In the name of Jesus, we pray. Amen.

For Further Reflection

1. What is your emotional response when you feel like the Lord is not hearing you?
2. What kinds of circumstances make you feel inclined to shut down?
3. What sorts of activities do you indulge in when you want to escape feeling that you are not heard?
4. Do you trust that God is always listening even when you do not feel His presence?

20 | His Love Makes the World Go Round

October 18, 2017

Whenever I am with Reagan, I tell her that I love her *so* much! And I also tell her that she makes my heart *so* happy! I have spoken those words and more—much more—since she was born. Affirmation is something with which she is well accustomed. After all, she is the prettiest, sweetest, smartest, most talented, and most loveable little four-year-old I know. She knows that Jesus loves her too, and when I tell her, she reminds me that Jesus lives in her heart. It is all so simple and so lovely!

One day as we were having our love ritual, Reagan informed me, "Actually everybody loves me, Nana!"

Yes, the people who know her do love her, and she loves the people who know her. But my natural inclination is to wonder when that ever-growing bubble will burst. As we all know, sometimes life is not that simple, not that easy, and not that lovely. And sorry to say, not everybody loves us.

We all want to protect childhood innocence as long as we can. It is such a precious time when everyone in the whole world loves you. How grateful I am that Reagan feels so secure about all the love around her and that she is beginning to understand about Jesus and His love for her. She is well aware that she is a child of God.

Isn't it something that even though we can't touch or see Jesus, we feel His love for us. A short time ago, Reagan asked me what Jesus looked like. We were at the chapel, and as I was about to try to answer her question, we noticed a picture of Him on the wall.

Without any hesitation, she loudly exclaimed, "Yes! Look! That's Jesus there. And look, Nana, His arms are out like a cross!"

She was so elated to see His picture. Her excitement about seeing the picture was also contagious for me. She is so open to knowing, loving, and trusting Him. She is genuinely enthusiastic about it! And so am I. Yet again, I am still allowing myself to entertain the thought, *How long will it last?* Right now, she is eager to learn and know all she can. But that's just the way it is when you are four. Right?

As we experience life, we have opportunities to learn important lessons. We can become hardened and jaded by our trials, or we can shake the dust off our proverbial sandals and move forward. We learn from the book of Matthew, "From the lips of children and infants, You have ordained praise." Yet as years pass by, why are we so quick to latch on to the ugly when life is not so pretty? What has happened to our lips of praise? We would do well to ask ourselves how we can "consider it pure joy whenever we face trials of many kinds" (James 1:2). The writings of James remind us that the "man who perseveres under trials, because he has stood the test, will receive the crown of life that God has promised to those who love him" (James 1:12).

Listening to what the world has to say only serves to confuse us. The voice of Our Creator is the only one we should be listening to and trusting in completely. He gives light to our path. When we truly believe that Jesus loves us, it really doesn't matter whether the rest of the world loves us or not. It is because of His love that He created this world, and it is His love that makes the world go round. We try to make that so complicated, but really it is so simple and so lovely!

Key Thought

His love makes the world go round.

Scripture

"When Jesus spoke again to the people, he said, 'I am the light of the world. Whoever follows me will never walk in darkness, but will have the light of life'" (John 8:12).

Prayer

Heavenly Lord, thank You for loving us so much. Thank You for the praises from the lips of children to remind us of Your unfailing love. Thank You for Your voice that speaks through the spirits of children, like sweet Reagan. Thank You for the joy that we all can experience when we listen, heed, and rejoice in You. Thank You for loving us, and thank You for Your love, which is the key to making the world go round. In Your name we pray. Amen.

For Further Reflection

1. When you hear the phrase "love makes the world go round," how do you respond?

2. How does your love for Jesus influence your view of the world?
3. How do you "consider it pure joy" when experiencing trials in your life? Be specific.
4. How does your conduct demonstrate you know you are a child of God and you are loved?

21 | Right Now

October 23, 2017

Reagan coughs a lot. She no longer seems to be bothered by it because it is so frequent. Most probably, it is a yet-to-be diagnosed allergy. She informed me, "Mommy says I should not eat ice cream or candy so then I won't cough so much." So my brilliant and obedient granddaughter has no problem cutting down on those things. Really? No ice cream and this four-year-old is okay with it? Whoa!

However, that strategy is not yet solving the problem. So naturally I worry about it. When I told her I was worried, she replied, "You don't need to worry about it, Nana. God is fixing my cough right now!" Her absolute certainty that the problem was being remedied honestly made me feel less anxious. Her total trust that she was being healed right now almost overwhelmed my heart.

Jesus plainly stated, "If you believe, you will receive whatever you ask for in prayer." It is right there in His Word. You believe; You receive. Regrettably, that is when the conversation too often becomes a complication.

Could I really just simply ask the Lord to heal Reagan's cough? Yes. Do I believe that He could easily cure her cough?

Yes. So why worry? What good does worrying do? None. In fact, it does more harm than good.

So then, what is my takeaway from this encounter? I will ask God to heal Reagan's cough, and I will take Reagan's sage advice to not worry about it. I will trust God to silence the buts and what-ifs going on in my head. I will thank Him for my hearing His voice through Reagan. And then Reagan and I will celebrate God's provision and enjoy a small ice cream cone.

Key Thought

Replace worry with trust.

Scripture

"If you believe, you will receive whatever you ask for in prayer" (Matthew 21:22).

Prayer

Thank You for the wisdom that Your child, Reagan, so confidently displayed. Help us all to receive what You have planned for us and know that it is for our good. We give You the glory and praise for being our Creator and Healer. Thank You that You make no mistakes. Thank You for the countless ways You display Your faithfulness toward us. May we always honor You for all that You are and all that You have done for us. In Christ's name we pray. Amen.

For Further Reflection

1. Do you believe that when you claim healing, you receive healing?

2. What are some concrete ways you can replace worry with trust?

3. If you keep a journal of prayer requests, how often have you reviewed your old requests and been amazed at all the Lord's answers?

4. Why do you think we often become disheartened when we don't get an answer right away, even though we trust God for the resolution?

His Eye Is on the Sparrow
Civilla D. Martin, Text
Charles H. Gabriel, Music
Public Domain

Based upon the text: *Are not five sparrows sold for two pennies? Yet not one of them is forgotten by God* (Luke 12:6)

Vs. 1—Why should I feel discouraged? Why should the shadows come? Why should my heart be lonely and long for heaven and home? When Jesus is my portion, my constant friend is He: His eye is on the sparrow and I know He watches me. His eye is on the sparrow and I know He watches me.

Vs. 2—"Let not your heart be troubled," His tender words I hear; And resting on His goodness, I lose my doubt and fear. Tho' by the path He leadeth, but one step I may see: His eye is on the sparrow and I know He watches me. His eye is on the sparrow and I know He watches me.

Refrain—I sing because I'm happy, I sing because I'm free; For His eye is on the sparrow and I know He watches me.

22 | The Rest of the Story

January 2, 2018

Recently my heart was pierced with Reagan's words, "Nana, the bad guys killed Jesus." When she made this declaration, we were riding in my car, and I seriously considered pulling off to the side of the road. How could I tell her in a simple way that there was much more to the story?

As I tried to explain that Jesus came back to life, she then naturally had more questions. "You mean only Jesus can come back to life? Where is He? He's in my heart? How?"

Soon however, her curiosity quelled, and she was equally emmeshed with explaining to me about *My Little Pony*, asking whether I knew the ponies' names. Then she continued on to tell me that she planned to be just like *Wonder Woman* when she got bigger. The moment had passed.

About two weeks later as I was dropping her back off to her daycare, I overheard a heated conversation between two four-year-old classmates. Again the dialogue stunned me. The little boy was raising his voice and insisting that (again) the bad guys killed Jesus and went on to emphatically explain that his dad told him that Jesus was dead.

A little was girl sitting across from him. With an anguished look on her face and in her voice, she replied, "My mom told me that Jesus is alive and He lives in our hearts."

Both children were equally adamant about what each parent had told them. The difference was that the little girl was hurt and the little boy was mad.

As I was walking out the door, I caught the eye of the little girl, nodded affirmingly to her, and mouthed the words, "Your mother is right. Jesus does live in your heart." I patted my heart, smiled at her, and felt very satisfied to witness her now-soothed spirit.

What children learn and hear sticks. Most of us remember singing "Jesus Loves Me" when we were young. We still sing it, and as we do, it resonates with a time when we had less knowledge, but we still believed that Jesus loved us. That simple childlike faith is something to be cherished. And it is something that can always serve to renew and revitalize our belief in the Savior who chose to die for us so we could live.

It seems to me that we need to stop, pull off the road, and take the time to explain the rest of the story every chance we get.

Key Thought

Take time to tell the greatest story of all.

Scripture

"Train up a child in the way he should go, and when he is old, he will not turn from it" (Proverbs 22:6).

Prayer

Thank You, Lord, for the honor and privilege to tell everyone we meet of Your great love for us. Please make us be alert to every opportunity to share the good news! Give us wisdom about when to speak, and may Your Holy Spirit guide our words for Your glory. We know that we are weak, but with Your strength, we can fulfill Your good purpose. Help us to be particularly sensitive to how we teach the young. Help us to glorify You with the rest of the story. In Your name we pray. Amen.

For Further Reflection

1. How bold are you to speak up when you hear conversation that is offensive concerning your beliefs?
2. When was the last time you had the opportunity to speak the truth about Jesus to a young person? What was the outcome?
3. What stops you from taking the time to pull off the road and explain more about the greatest story of all?
4. Who has had the greatest impact upon your faith life? Share some significant details.

23 | Cracked But Not Broken

January 10, 2018

So many amazing conversations happen when Reagan and I are in the car coming and going to different fun places. We are always looking forward to our new adventure. Maybe that is why our dialogue is so dynamic and engaging. We are tuned into each other and looking forward to our day together. Reagan will often start our discussions with words like, "Nana, I want to talk about …" Usually she wants to talk about her daycare friends or her favorite toys.

On this particular day, she wanted to talk about her heart. She started the conversation with, "You know Mommy broke my heart." Yes, she had told me that before, so I was not as startled by the comment this time. Reagan then went on to explain to me that she loved her friend Luke "so much." Well, yes, I told her I already knew that too, but what I really wasn't expecting was her next comment.

"You know, Nana, I said Mommy broke my heart, but I still love Luke so much. So my heart must not be broken … it is just cracked."

Wow! Yes, there are things that hurt and disappoint us, and those are cracks. Through our lives we experience all kinds of trials that cause those cracks. Some are deep and wide; others are momentary. Cracks happen regularly. How we deal with them becomes the issue.

For now, little Reagan can be satisfied and comforted to know that Jesus lives in her heart and He will take care of those cracks. If only, with the same childlike faith, we could yield to that simple, yet incredibly awesome, power and truth. Our Lord not only heals, restores, and renews, He also protects, fills, and causes joy to overflow in our hearts beyond our imagination. This happens when we invite Him in to do His work in us. He is the healer of our hearts, cracks and all.

Key Thought

Jesus is the healer of our hearts.

Scripture

"He heals the brokenhearted and binds up their wounds" (Psalm 147:3).

Prayer

Dear heavenly Father, it is our desire that You reign in our hearts always and under all circumstances. Sometimes when we are hurting, we allow our cracks to rule. Please help us to remember that You are sovereign over all matters of the heart. May the joy of knowing You bring us comfort during trials. May we trust that You know all about whatever we are going through and You are in charge. Thank You for the cracks that teach us lessons, and thank You for the cracks that You repair. Thank You for Your love that binds all wounds. In the healing name of Jesus, we pray. Amen.

For Further Reflection

1. Do you believe that Jesus can completely heal our broken hearts?
2. Why do you think that many people seem to hold on to the cracks even though they say they believe that Jesus can heal them?
3. How would you personally define the word "love"?
4. Think of the people in your life whom you love, and make a concerted effort to thank them this week. As you do this, thank God for the joy of loving.

> **"And now here is my secret: It is only with the heart that one can see rightly; what is essential is invisible to the eye."**
> —Antoine de Saint-Exupéry, *The Little Prince*

24 | Family

January 26, 2018

Recently I went to pick up my son and Reagan to go to a restaurant so we could enjoy lunch together. As I came in the door, Reagan met me and very proudly said, "This is my dad. You haven't met him."

At first, I was startled and feebly attempted to start to explain that indeed I knew him. But I stopped quickly, and my son and I just chuckled. It was funny! Kids don't always remember about how people are related, and my son had been away a long time working in another state.

A few days later, Reagan proudly told me that she and her parents had rebuilt their porch together.

"You know, Nana, we all did it together … you know, like a family."

While Daddy was home, this project was very important to her because they all did it together. She was beaming with pride as she spoke about being a family.

When Daddy was away, Reagan and I talked about the fact that he is my son, and she seemed to understand that very well—in theory. But when he was back home and we were all together, the dots just did not seem to connect that Nana was his momma.

Whether our family relationships are strong or weak, they are a big part of who we are, and they impact our lives in countless ways. We can all relate to doing things in spite of or because of family relationships. All too often, we view and describe family matters as complicated.

The same may be true of our relationship with Jesus. We frequently experience a spectrum of emotions about Him. When we feel detached from Him or when we are not hearing His voice, we can mistakenly think, *I do not know Him*, or *He must not know me*. Again, we know, in theory, that is not true, but it still may be what we are feeling and even be what we may actually say.

During those times, we need not to chuckle but to commit to time together, free from distractions, and gratefully remember, "He is my Father, and I am His cherished child." And yes, right now, I may feel like He does not know me, but I know better. We are family.

Key Thought

Family matters.

Scripture

"He is the Father of all who believe" (Romans 4:11).

Prayer

Dear heavenly Father, thank You for knowing us and loving us. What a great privilege it is to be part of the family of God and heirs in Your kingdom. When we forget or do not acknowledge You the way we should, we humbly ask for forgiveness. Please help us to have wisdom about family matters, and may our counsel be from You, only You. Being Your child in the family of God is the greatest blessing of all. Thank you, dear heavenly Father. Amen.

For Further Reflection

1. When the Lord is referred to as "Father," what is your response?
2. How would you describe the relationships in your nuclear family?
3. Is it important for you to have strong family relationships? If so, what do you do to support that bond?
4. How does knowing that you are a child of God make you feel?

> **"Love is measured not in moments of time… but in timeless moments."**
>
> —Robert W. Lawrence

Carol Hamblet Adams, *My Beautiful Sandcastle Moments*, Harvest House Publishers, 2004.

25 | Sharing Everyday Blessings

March 28, 2018

Recently I have found myself listening with attentive ears, trying to try to catch cute things Reagan might say. With my newfound nugget, I then would have something to write about that was fresh and different. But the sad truth is that those endearing, innocent responses are becoming less frequent. How can I continue to write my book without Reagan's delightful input? That curious dilemma has prompted me to think about the everyday conversations that are not particularly astoundingly insightful or even mildly adorable, but they are always engaged.

Every week, Reagan and I are in the car to go to music class or the pool, and we always talk on the way. She often will say, "Let's talk about what we see, Nana." We then play a game of, "I spy with my little eye," and we find something to fill in the blank with what we see. Because of this little game, she has learned to read speed limit signs, and she knows the color of interstate signs. She also points out to me the bike lane signs and takes great interest in and tells me every time how billowy the steam is coming out at the local electric plant. In other words, the everyday things that are nothing new to me unexpectedly take on new meaning.

More importantly, we are also making great use of our time in the car together: We are communicating. We are having fun, and I find myself trying to spot the yellow or blue sign first so I can say

I saw it first. But no, she will laugh and talk even louder than I do, name the sign, and declare that she is the winner. Then with no hesitation at all, she will say, "Actually we both win, Nana." Now there is the real gold nugget right there! We both win.

My quest to write a book and Reagan's desire to learn are important, but not nearly as important as our connection with one another. We love each other, and sharing conversations with each other increasingly strengthens the bond we share. I think Reagan already knows that or she wouldn't so spontaneously tell me that we both win. We want the best for each other. Together, we are winners.

I watch her in my rearview mirror and must be careful not to tarry too long observing her. As I shift my eyes from looking in the mirror at Reagan to actually paying attention to the road as I drive, I think that Jesus must, to some extent, do the same thing. He knows what is ahead, but He is also keeping an eye on us where we are right now. We feel His delight when we have learned something that He wants us to know. And His desire to be in relationship with us is something that is always and forever. He knows our past, our present, and our future. As we seek to grow spiritually and better understand how to apply the teachings in His Word, our relationship deepens. We may not fully understand everything, but that is okay. Staying in relationship is what is important.

During our trips together, Reagan has spied with her little eye lots of things that are both old and new. It never gets tiresome because we are sharing the time together. The everyday blessings that we may have taken for granted become less mundane and more valued because they are shared.

Key Thought

Sharing together is always a win.

Scripture

"Above all, love each other deeply" (1 Peter 4:8).

Prayer

Heavenly Lord, thank You that You are our Friend. Thank You that You make all things new. Thank You for the everyday blessings that are so abundant that sometimes we can't see them. Please help us to keep our eyes open, Lord, to all that You would have us see. Thank You for the greatest blessing of all, which is experiencing them with You. With grateful hearts, we pray, and thank You, Lord Jesus. Amen.

For Further Reflection

1. Can you name some everyday occurrences that you take for granted?
2. Think of an example of an experience that took on new meaning when it was shared.
3. Have you felt the Lord's delight concerning His relationship with you? Describe it.
4. How attuned do you think you are to hear what the Lord wants you to know?

"One of the most influential handclasps is that of a grandparent around the hand of a grandchild."
—Robert Strand, *Moments for Grandparents*, New Leaf Press, 1994.

26 | Winners

April 12, 2018

For three years, we have enjoyed an Easter egg hunt tradition that has been fun, revealing, and memory-making. This year was no exception. We have quite a collection of wooden Easter eggs that Bampa has ordered from the White House. The eggs sit on a shelf in our house all year long, and when the egg hunt day arrives, it is always a happy, much-anticipated time. We customarily put the eggs all around the living room and den areas, usually in plain view, and Reagan hurriedly and excitedly collects them in her basket until there are no more to be found. Then we repeat the sequence over and over again. She loves collecting the eggs and counting them, and she does not seem to care at all that they are wooden eggs and not chocolate. I have to wonder how long that will last.

This year, we again hid the eggs for her, and she gleefully picked them up. And then about the third time around, she suggested that she should hide them and we should find them. She took great care hiding them, and then as we tried to find them, she started pointing out where they were to help us. We had modeled that for her, so the fact that she was doing the same for us was not a big surprise.

However, her next suggestion was rather startling. Reagan

thoughtfully suggested, "Nana and Bampa, I think we should all hide the eggs together, and then we will all find them together." I thought to myself that we could do that even though I wanted to explain to her that if we hid them, then we would already know where to find them.

I did not say anything, and we started gathering our eggs. Reagan was faster gathering the eggs than we were, and when she saw that she had more eggs than we did, she again started helping us by pointing out where the eggs were. She then explained, "We all need to win, Nana."

I thought, *Okay, Reagan, we all need to win.* I thanked her for helping us, and we proceeded to count our eggs. She had ten; we had ten. We all won, and it was a much bigger win than just having the same number of eggs.

It amazes me that in this day and age of "that's mine and more is better" Reagan's attention was on us all winning. Her heart was happy, and her beaming smile revealed that wanting the best for Bampa and me was the big win. How wonderful it would be if that attitude could be evident throughout all of our comings and goings in life. Yes, competition is great, and winning is fun, but I am referring to the way we treat each other every day. What if we actually encouraged everyone around us every single day and literally told them that they were winners?

That concept is not a foreign one to me. My father, Bill Denison, consistently told me throughout my entire life that I was a winner and I could do anything I wanted to do. He would go on to say that he would always support me if what I wanted to do was honorable. He said the exact same thing to my two sisters. Breathing that kind of life into people is the big win! And at four years old, Reagan already knows that! God sees us all as winners, and we win each time we help each other win.

Key Thought

We all win when we are serving others.

Scripture

"Whoever wants to become great among you must be your servant" (Matthew 20:26).

Prayer

Dear heavenly Lord, once again, out of the mouth of a babe, You have revealed Your truth. Thank You for loving us and wanting the best for each of us. Thank You that You see us as winners. Please help us to know how to serve one another in ways that bring You glory. In Your strength, may we stay focused on what You would have us pursue. Thank You for the beautiful reminder from Reagan about what winning really means. In the powerful name of Christ Jesus, we pray. Amen.

For Further Reflection

1. Are you competitive to a fault? Explain.
2. Are you an encourager?
3. Do you feel like a winner?
4. Has there been a time in your life when your competitive attitude was harmful to another person? Explain how you did or did not resolve the situation.

Image by Megan Denison Smith @2019

27 | Mistakes and Accidents

July 28, 2018

Reagan and I had waited all summer to finally be able to arrange a time when we could go to the pool. Our summer schedules were just not jiving to have our long-anticipated fun day together. But finally on July 28, we made it happen! When we arrived, we learned that a child had unfortunately had an accident in the outdoor pool and that it was going to be closed for cleaning. No problem, there was also a great indoor children's pool, so we headed on over there.

The indoor pool has several different water slides to choose from: small, medium, and large. Reagan has graduated to the medium slide and goes down all by herself now. She knows how to dodge the bucket of water that tries to douse each child as they climb the steps to the entrance of the slide. On this day, because the outdoor pool was temporarily closed, there were lots and lots of kids going down the slides.

Reagan enjoyed going on the slide, but about the fifth time down, there was a mishap. The older boy who went down the slide ahead of her decided to play at the bottom of the slide rather than get out of the way for the next descending child. Since the slide was enclosed, there was no way to see him at the bottom. You just had to take your chances that the previous child was quick enough to get out of the way. No such luck! Reagan came swirling down the slide. Boom! They collided.

Reagan tearfully came over to me at the side of the pool. Her feelings were hurt more than her body was. I told her that I was so sorry about the accident. At that point, she stopped her whimpering, looked me straight in the eyes, and adamantly informed me, "No, Nana, that was not an accident. That was a mistake. It was not an accident."

I thought about that. The boy had made a mistake by staying at the bottom of the slide too long. He did not get out of the way, and that resulted in an accident. A mistake can be intentional or unintentional. It was obvious that Reagan wanted to make it very clear that the boy made a mistake and she did not. He caused the accident intentionally.

Okay, so what is the lesson here? We all make mistakes, and sometimes our mistakes hurt people. Perhaps the lesson is that we should pay more attention to what we are doing and be more focused on how our actions may impact others. The little boy was preoccupied playing at the bottom of the slide, and yet he knew there were lots of other kids behind him coming down.

We all do the same thing to greater and lesser degrees with varying levels of awareness. Immediately the example of managing time comes to my mind. When groups or individuals are supposed to meet at a certain time, there are always the stragglers. We know who they are, and we know that they are always going to be late. We expect it. It is not exactly an accident, but the waiting does sometimes actually hurt the group.

Of course, mistakes can be unintentional, and very often an accident may result. Many driving accidents are a great example of that. Because we want to avoid a car accident, we take certain precautions. We choose to have a heightened awareness to try to avoid an accident. Yet some people intentionally run red lights or drive impaired and think only about themselves and how they can get away with it. They fail to factor in how their poor judgment can potentially harm others.

Carefully considering the differences between accidents and intentional mistakes that cause them is something we could all benefit from practicing. On a spiritual level, we can apply some assertions that should make us very uncomfortable. It is an intentional mistake to not put Christ first. It is an intentional mistake to not adopt a lifestyle that demonstrates our priorities. It is an intentional mistake to think it is okay to put our desires before His desires for us. When we intentionally do these things, the consequences are not accidents. They are absolutely the consequences of our intentional mistakes.

How often have we uttered statements like, "I know I shouldn't say this" or "I know I shouldn't do this, but ..." We all have long lists of things we actually say or think that are intentional mistakes. This then begs the question, "How many accidents could be avoided if we consistently and intentionally chose to invite the Lord to guide our thoughts and our actions?"

Reagan was right. The boy made a mistake. This was another life lesson from the Lord spoken through her. If we deliberately choose to make the conscious decision to get out of the way, there would be a lot less accidents.

Key Thought

Get out of the way!

Scripture

"In all your ways acknowledge him, and He will make your paths straight" (Proverbs 3:6).

Prayer

So many times, Lord, I have chosen to pursue my own desires and neglected to invite You to guide my way. Please forgive me, Lord. Thank you, Lord, for knowing me, loving me, and teaching me that Your ways are perfect. Please put the desire in all of our hearts to be more intentional about our actions. May our choices bring glory and honor to You. Help us to listen and hear Your voice as we go up and down the slides of life. In Your name we pray. Amen.

For Further Reflection

1. Are you able to name times when you intentionally have done something wrong, thinking no one would get hurt and yet they were?
2. How would you explain the differences between an accident and a mistake?
3. Why do you think it was so important to Reagan to explain the difference between mistakes and accidents?
4. Is it your habit to invite the Lord to guide your actions, or are you more inclined to listen to your own thoughts? Explain.

"Guide Me O Thou Great Jehovah"
William Williams, Text; John Hughes, Music

Vs. 1—Guide me, O Thou great Jehovah, Pilgrim through this barren land; I am week but Thou art mighty; Hold me with thy powerful hand; Bread of heaven, Bread of heaven, feed me till I want no more. Feed me till I want no more.

Vs. 2—Open now the crystal fountain, Whence the healing stream doth flow; Let the fire and cloudy pillar lead me all the journey through; Strong Deliverer, strong Deliverer, Be Thou still my strength and shield, Be Thou still my strength and shield.

28 | You Better Watch Out!

August 11, 2018

There is a great amusement park that has lots and lots of rides that are perfect for little kids. It is called Santa's Workshop, and it is in the foothills near Colorado Springs, just up the road from the famous Garden of the Gods Park. Reagan and I had planned to have a wonderful day together, driving up the mountain and going on the rides. On the way there, she reminded me that the one thing she did not want to do was see Santa.

Just about a year ago, we were having a grand time at Santa's Workshop, and while we were there, Reagan peeked in the door and saw Santa. She immediately turned around and ran for her life. I found her hiding behind Santa's house. So this year, when she announced that she did not want to see Santa, I did not push the subject … much. As we were walking past his workshop, I gently suggested that it might be nice to just peek in the door to see what he looked like. We did that and then hastily moved on to the next ride.

After about five hours of either watching the kiddie rides or squeezing into the kiddie seats for a ride with Reagan, we both decided that it might be a good idea to head home. As we were winding our way back to the entrance, we passed Santa's house, and who came out the door but Mr. and Mrs. Claus. There we were face-to-face with them, and Reagan put her head down, crossed her arms, and literally froze. Santa tried to engage with her, but there was no way she was going to respond to him.

I picked up all lanky thirty-eight pounds of her and said it was okay. "You know Santa loves kids!" There was no taking the bait. Mr. and Mrs. Claus went on their way, and Reagan then stated that she needed to go on four more rides and then we could leave.

I remember being scared of my elementary school principal, a very nice, kind, and gentle man. As I got older, I was also skittish around others who were important. So I suppose it was not unusual for Reagan to be afraid of Santa. Perhaps the beard is a bit scary. It is interesting to note though that Reagan sings "Santa Claus Is Coming to Town" year-round. She definitely expects presents from him. But to actually meet him, no way!

This little scenario reminded me again of the song introduced by Mercy Me entitled "I Can Only Imagine." The beautiful lyrics ask questions about how we think we will respond when we see Jesus. Will we dance, stand in awe, or be still? I think it is a good thing to think about regularly. Is there a way to prepare for that glorious day? Probably our best choice is to live as He would have us live.

Of course, there is a world of difference between Santa Claus and Jesus. But I think that sometimes we think that we better watch out, we better not cry, we better not pout, and this is why because Jesus is coming to town. We deceive ourselves into believing that we have to be good in order for Jesus to love us. We operate out of a base of fear rather than freedom in Him.

I don't know why Reagan does not want to see Santa, but I know she knows he loves her. I don't know why we act like Jesus is not coming to town because He is and it could be today! I also don't know how I will respond when I see Him. But one thing is for sure: I am going to keep my watch out for Him in my everyday comings and goings. And I will remember that when I run, He is still with me. When I freeze, He holds me. That's more than Santa ever thought about doing.

Key Thought

You better watch out!

Scripture

"Watch and pray so that you will not fall into temptation. The spirit is willing but the body is weak" (Matthew 26:41).

Prayer

I can only imagine what it will be like to see You face-to-face, Lord. Until that day comes, help me to live the life that demonstrates freedom in You. Thank You for knowing me, loving me, protecting me, and blessing me in ways that are too numerous to even know. In Christ's name, I pray. Amen.

For Further Reflection

1. What do you think your response will be when you see Jesus face-to-face?
2. Do you think that some people operate more out of a base of fear rather than freedom in Christ? Explain.
3. How does your life reflect that you enjoy freedom in Christ?
4. Are you ready for Jesus to come to town today?

First Christmas with Bampa, Nana, and Reagan

29 | Being a Butterfly—Only

August 15, 2018

As Reagan and I were riding in the car today, another golden time of conversation took place. I picked her up from daycare because she was not feeling well. But whatever malady she was experiencing certainly did not detract her from making some very thought-provoking comments.

The dialogue began like this. "Nana, I would like to be something that flies." *Yes, that would be nice*, I thought. *You could go anywhere unimpeded and see so many things.* So I asked her if she would like to be a bird or even an airplane. She responded very quickly with, "No, Nana, I would like to be a butterfly." I then asked her what color she would be, and she said her colors would be like a rainbow. That sounded very lovely, so I asked where she would go.

And then came the zinger! She replied, "I would fly to all the different flowers and sit on the petals and smell them."

What a lovely thought! I was reminded of the commonly used phrase that bids us to stop and smell the roses. To think, here is an almost five-year-old who has all the toys she could want and is as busy as a bee, and she is thinking about perching on petals and smelling the different fragrances of flowers. How lovely!

Reagan proceeded to qualify her wish by adding that she really did not want to be a caterpillar first. She just wanted to be a butterfly. My thoughts then swiftly shifted to thinking that many of us have rose-colored glasses when we are young. We want to experience the sights and smells that are new and exciting. Yet it is that caterpillar stage that tends to trap us—hopefully not for too long.

We all have different ideas about what makes life sweet. For some, doing things like smelling flowers breathes life into our days. Our colors become naturally more radiant as we do. Whatever it takes to add meaning to our days, we would be well advised to make it a priority. Being a caterpillar first grows our wings so we are able to fly to find those flowers. If we embrace that struggle rather than try to resist or deny it, we are always stronger for it.

But for today, I feel satiated by the beauty of the idea that my dear granddaughter's imagination has fluttered to a place where smelling flowers is what she would like to do. That simple, beautiful image of being a butterfly so you can smell flowers is a place where the fragrance of the Lord abounds.

Key Thought

Smelling flowers breathes life into our days.

Scripture

"Come see what the Lord has done, how awesome His works in man's behalf!" (Psalm 66:5).

Prayer

Thank You, Lord, for all the beauty around us and for the detail of it all. The fragrance of Your presence is sweeter than anything on this earth. We have a glimpse of Your loveliness as we enjoy the sights and smells of flowers. Father God, we thank You for gracing this earth with such abundant bouquets of beauty. Help us to linger more often with You in the garden You have so generously provided for us. We humbly thank You. In Christ's Name we pray. Amen.

For Further Reflection

1. What adds beauty to your day?
2. Have you ever literally experienced the fragrance of the Lord? If you have, describe it!
3. In what ways do you bless others with the gifts God has given to you?
4. Share how a caterpillar stage was beneficial to your life, and give God the glory for it.

30 | Yes, My Heart Is Leaping for Joy Too!

August 23, 2018

Reagan and I talk a lot about our hearts when we are riding in the car. A lot! Reagan always wants to hear about how our being together makes my heart happy. Today was no exception. The dialogue went something like this.

"Nana, ask me what makes your heart happy."

"Okay, Reagan, what makes my heart happy?"

"You say that being with me makes your heart happy."

"Yes, that's right, Reagan. Being with you makes my heart happy."

"Being with you makes my heart happy too, Nana. Now let's say it again, Nana."

As this delightful little ritual was repeated a couple more times, it was apparent that Reagan wanted me to add something about our happy hearts. And then she did. "Nana, don't you want to tell me that your happy heart is jumping for joy too?"

Yep! My happy heart, for sure, was jumping for joy. I had told her that in times past, and she had remembered. Obviously it was important for her to hear it again.

How many times have we heard stories of people who were never told that they were loved? All too often we hear about the regret felt when they were never able to hear words that could have made such a difference in their lives.

I tell my little one how much I love her and how special she is every single time I see her. She knows that her Nana adores her, but she also wants to hear it. We can all relate to that. Just because we know something does not mean that we don't want to hear it.

When my dearly departed daddy wrote to me or spoke to me on the phone, he always ended with, "You know, honey, I adore you." Yes, I knew it, and I felt adored by him. And I loved hearing him say it. I have an entire three-ring binder filled with emails that he sent to me. I printed them off and saved all of them because I wanted to read those three words, "I adore you."

God wants to hear that we love Him too. He knows it already, but that is not the point. We need to say it, and we need to hear ourselves say it. We need to say that our hearts are leaping for joy because we love Him. He is with us all the time, and that should be enough to want to tell Him all the time!

I am not always with Reagan, but I do carry her in my heart all the time. The next time I am with her, I will be certain to remember to tell her that my heart is happy and leaping for joy.

Key Thought

Even though you know it, it is also great to hear it and to say it.

Scripture

"From the lips of children and infants you have ordained praise" (Psalm 8:2a).

Prayer

Thank You, dear Lord, for reminding me, through Reagan, that speaking words of praise is important! You are so gracious to remind us that words matter! Hear our words of adoration and know that You are our sovereign Lord. Thank You for loving us! Thank You for adoring us! Please help us to remember to acknowledge You for Your greatness! Our hearts leap for joy when we consider all that You are! You are the great I Am, and we give You praise forever and always! In Christ's name we pray. Amen.

For Further Reflection

1. Who do you adore? How often do you share those words?
2. Do you feel adored by someone? If so, describe the feeling.
3. Do you know that the Lord adores you?
4. Praise is wonderful to receive as well as to give. In what ways could you commit to offer more words of praise to others?

31 | New in Christ

July 23, 2018

It has been my long-held belief that as we do things like writing and singing, we are always enriched by the process. The end product may not be the best we had hoped for, but the endeavor was definitely the prize. As a music therapist, I have used my skills to primarily work with the elderly. I was privileged and blessed to serve them as an activity professional for over twenty years. For the most part, people love music, so when I officially retired, I decided that the music would not stop. Once a month, I have committed to present a music program at an assisted living home.

On this particular day, it was a double dip of blessing that my granddaughter accompanied me. I explained to her that we were going to a home where very, very old people lived. I continued on to tell her that the people would be much older than I. In Reagan's eyes, her nana is very, very old! She shook her head and nodded that she understood.

As we were talking about age, Reagan then proceeded to explain to me that she understood that the people would be very old, but then added, "You know, Nana, they are old, but I am new."

New! I love it! I very briefly considered following up by

explaining the differences between the words "young" and "new," but then I immediately knew that the Lord wanted me to hear the word "new."

New. New. New.

Wouldn't it be fantastic if we all thought of ourselves as new? Because we really are! We are all new creatures in Christ, and if we all chose to live that way every day, wouldn't it be wonderful? Actually I am believing that is the message that the Lord has been delivering to me throughout this journey of writing these meditations. Reagan has been a light for me to shine His glory as a new creature in Christ!

Reagan's simple, innocent comments have all provided glimpses of Himself. How I have loved growing with Reagan! Now it is time to conclude this little book of meditations and to spread the light of His glory to others. As new creatures in Christ, we are His Light.

Key Thought

Live knowing we are new in Christ each day!

Scripture

"Therefore, if anyone is in Christ, he is a new creation; the old has gone, the new has come!" (2 Corinthians 5:17).

Prayer

Thank You, Lord, that we are all brand new in You! Thank You for the privilege to share Your good news and for the variety of ways You choose to speak to us. Thank You for using my precious granddaughter to help me hear Your voice. May

Your Light now shine through these writings for others to see Your glory. In Christ's name I pray. Amen.

For Further Reflection

1. Do you conduct your life as a new creation in Christ? How?
2. Why do you think some people have such trouble seeing themselves as new in Christ?
3. Describe ways you have been blessed to be a blessing.
4. His divine direction is the light for our lives and our world. Share how you will explore new ways to share His light for His good purpose and begin today.

Image by Megan Denison Smith@2019

Epilogue

We are all children of God, and with Christ, we are heirs of God's glory. Years ago, I wrote a song that I am sharing with you now. The lyrics encapsulate the intent of this meditation book. May we all seek to grow in the Lord and especially take advantage of every opportunity to guide the young. This song has been sung many times for baptisms for our family members and others. It reminds us of who we are and what our responsibilities are to guide new followers of Christ.

Child of God

Chorus—Child of God, angel of light, God holds you gently with care. Go with God in peace always from now on with His love.

Vs. 1—You are a child of promise! You are a child of joy! God will provide and always be there for you!

Vs. 2—Now for you, (insert your name), we pledge to be your guides. God will light the way. Walk with the Lord!

Vs. 3—You are a child of love, dedicated to Christ, our Lord! Let Him grow in your heart. God loves you so!

Words and lyrics by Deborah Denison Bailey, Copyright 1993.

End Notes

All scriptures are taken from the *Women of Faith Study Bible*, New International Version, Copyright @2001 by the Zondervan Corporation, Library of Congress Number 00-133720.

Historical quotes are taken from *Christianity Today* 2019, unless otherwise noted. Public Domain.

The Celebration Hymnal, Songs and Hymns for Worship was used for lyrics for "His Eye Is on the Sparrow" and "Guide Me, O Thou Great Jehovah." Copyright 1997 by Word Music/ Integrity Music. Lyrics are Public Domain.

About the Author

Deborah (Debbie) Denison Bailey has enjoyed a distinguished career as a gifted musician in many different venues and capacities. Her hobbies include writing, composing, gardening, walking, traveling, and beaching. She has been blessed with enduring friendships, including her marriage of forty-five years to Paul. They have a son, a daughter, and a granddaughter, Reagan, and they live in Colorado Springs, Colorado.

Deborah Denison Bailey

Printed in the United States
By Bookmasters